The Greater in Me

by Lori Wilson

Illustrations by Reginald Byers

WestBow Press books may be ordered through booksellers or by contacting:

WestBow Press
A Division of Thomas Nelson & Zondervan
1663 Liberty Drive
Bloomington, IN 47403
www.westbowpress.com
1 (866) 928-1240

Illustrations by Reginald Byers

ISBN: 978-1-5127-1672-6 (sc)
ISBN: 978-1-5127-1671-9 (e)

Library of Congress Control Number: 2015918667

Print information available on the last page.

WestBow Press rev. date: 12/18/2015

WESTBOW
PRESS®
A DIVISION OF THOMAS NELSON
& ZONDERVAN

This book is lovingly dedicated to:

Cameron, Jake, Jeremiah, & Saya

- The "Dream Team"

Once upon a time in a place far, far, away... (Yeah, you're right, that's way too cliché.)

This
isn't a fairy tale.
It's just
a real simple
story, about
a real little
person, searching for
her glory.

**When Daddy left,
I was only three...**

and I blamed me.

Maybe if I were **taller?**

Maybe if I were
smaller?

Maybe if
I didn't make
so much
noise
when I played...

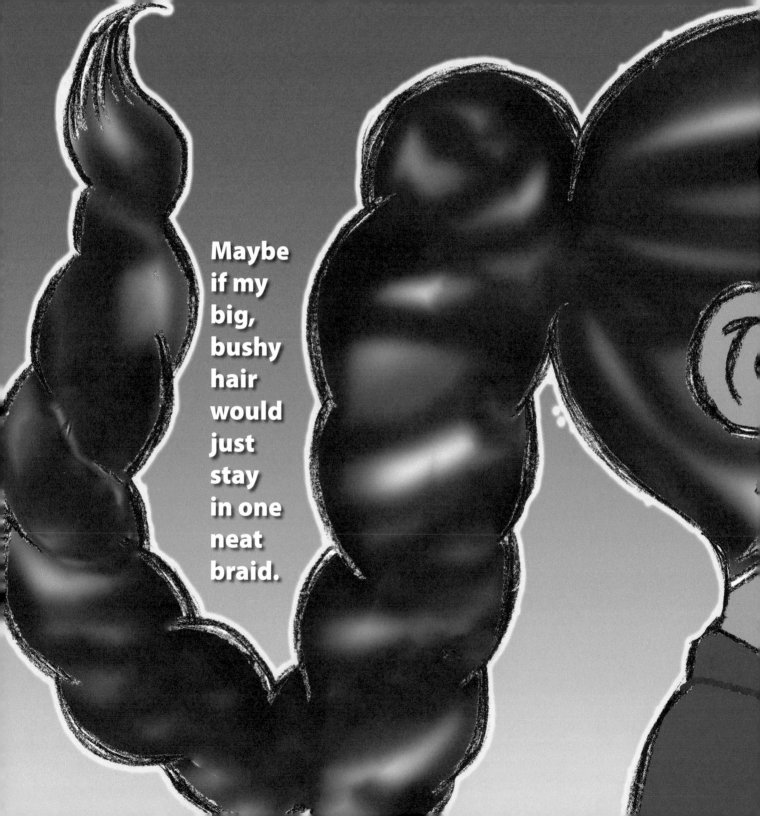

Maybe if my big, bushy hair would just stay in one neat braid.

or a less picky eater? Then, maybe he would have stayed.

But he didn't. **He left.**

As soon as the door closed behind him, I started my journey...

Not having him there really hurt. But it also started me on my search.

If I could find what made me special, maybe I wouldn't feel so sad…

When I saw other boys and girls spending time with their Dads.

Or better yet...

Maybe he would **change his mind?!?!**

Wishing he would knock on the door and say he made a **mistake,**

And instead of his things, it was **me** he would take!

But that didn't happen.

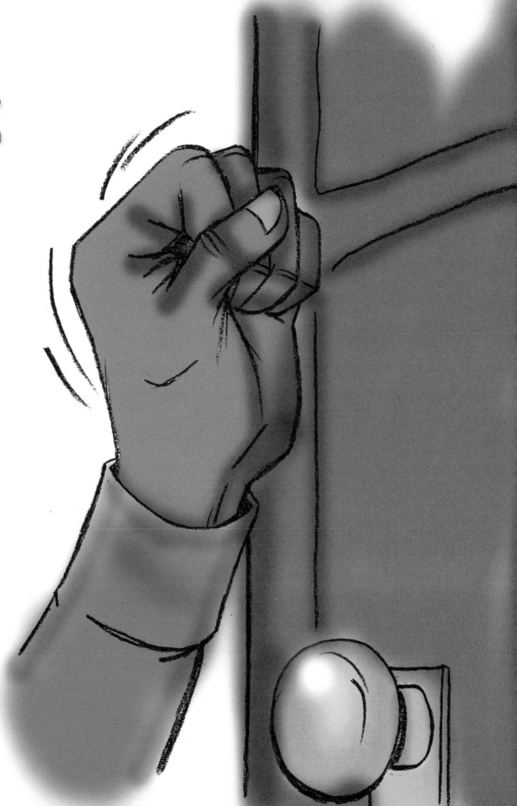

Sometimes I would get mad and **yell** for no reason.

I stopped studying, talked back to my Mom, and even quit soccer for a season.

I started looking at other kids like they were better than me.

They seemed smarter, more popular...and they had a daddy.

Well, that was all I needed to help me see, that I still had to find the "greater" in me.

There must be something that makes me stand out.

Something that would make people shout:

"WOW! That kid is really S-P-E-C-I-A-L!!!"

I loved to sing, but EVERYONE agreed, it wasn't my thing.

I loved to run, but wasn't very fast. As a matter of fact,

I finished last.

But I had to find the "greater" in me.

Maybe if I told jokes like they did on TV, the other kids would laugh **with** me.

knock knock
who's there?
orange
orange who?
orange you glad I'm
not a banana!

When no
one laughed,
it was easy
to see,
that comedy
was NOT the
thing for me.

My teacher couldn't help me,
neither could my brother.

Not friends, not Daddy,
not even my mother.

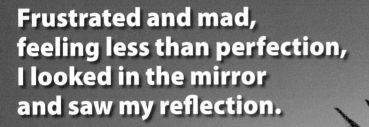

Frustrated and mad,
feeling less than perfection,
I looked in the mirror
and saw my reflection.

My MESSY hair,
my CHUBBY cheeks,
those are things that

make me **unique.**
It took a mirror to help me see,
it's what's **INSIDE**
that's the "greater" in me.

It was as if God's love turned on a light.
I went from sad, to knowing I was **MORE** than alright. And even with a chipped tooth, and crooked smile, the "greater" in me had been there **all the while!**

The "greater" in me was way **MORE** than people could see.

It was my love for others and my corny jokes,
it was my big laugh, my short stubby toes;
it was my way of always seeing the glass half full
it was the fact that I like cookies and orange juice in a bowl.

God created me unique, with a purpose in mind;
it was what it took me a long time to find.
after thinking, wondering, and searching I see,
the "greater" in me

- IS ME!!

I still love my Daddy, even though he lives far away.

He told me that I'll always be his baby, even if he doesn't see me every day.

Today I know that I am:

Funny,
Bright,
I can settle
disagreements
without a fight,
Strong,
Creative,
Beautiful,
Smart,
My friends like to
spend time with
me,
and my future is
full of possibility,

because I've found the "greater" in me!

What about **YOU? YOU** are special too!

Now, make your own list of reasons why you're special, and remind yourself of those reasons every day!
Start your list by picking from the following qualities:

smart	kind	patient
bold	peaceful	good leader
caring	sense of humor	good follower
thoughtful	good handwriting	determined
strong	good helper	see the good
funny	good at sharing	in others
loving	encourage others	optimistic
	big smile	friendly

Here is what you can do every morning, and every night before bed- choose one quality and

say it out loud 10 times,

like: "I am smart!"

and really believe it!

See how special YOU are? GOD loves YOU - and so do I!

Printed in the United States
By Bookmasters